and Carol Raycraft

ntry and Folk Antiques

WITH PRICE GUIDE

Schiffer Publishing Ltd

77 Lower Valley Road, Atglen, PA 19310

Printed in Hong Kong

ISBN: 0-88740-828-1

Library of Congress Cataloging-in-Publication Data

Raycraft, Don.
    Country and folk antiques/Don and Carol Raycraft.
        p. cm.
    ISBN 0-88740-828-1 (paper)
    1. General stores--Collectibles--United States--
Catalogs. I. Raycraft, Carol. II. Title.
NK807.R384 1995
745.1'0973'075--dc20   95-18997
                    CIP

Published by Schiffer Publishing, Ltd.
77 Lower Valley Road
Atglen, PA 19310
write for a free catalog.
This be purchased from the publisher.
Please include $2.95 postage.
Try your bookstore first.

We are interested in hearing from authors
with book ideas on related subjects.

Contents

Introduction 5

Chapter 1   Kitchen Antiques 11

Chapter 2   Stonewares 33

Chapter 3   Country Furniture 56

Chapter 4   Country Store Antiques 79

Chapter 5   Baskets 109

Chapter 6   Toys 120

Chapter 7   "A Little Bit About a Lot of Things" 139

Chapter 8   Country Christmas 152

              Price Guide 159

Early nineteenth century grandfather's clock, pine and poplar, found in Indiana. Mid-nineteenth century painted spindle-back bench decorated with poinsettias.

Acknowledgments

We would like to thank the individuals and couples whose names appear below for their assistance in bringing this project to fruition. Without their cooperation and good humor it could not have been completed.

Douglas Congdon-Martin
Ken and Carlene Elliott
Bernie and Jerry Green
Todd and Marlene Harting
Dr. Alex Hood
Brenda Humphrey
Karla Mergen
Walter Lash
Opal Pickens
Kathy and Russ Pribble
Jetsy and Steve Sachtleben
Peter Schiffer
Connie Shiever
Richard and Vanessa Wayne
Manuela Yokota

Introduction

The standard line that Americana collectors confront is that the "good stuff" is gone and it is a waste of time to look because "it's just not out there anymore." There is some isolated truth to the above, if you are using shop inventories or auction catalogues from the 1950s or 1960s as your road map. In reality, though, significant collections are still being assembled. Today it calls for deeper pockets, more time, and some knowledge. Yesterday it took a checkbook and a truck to haul the stuff home.

It is also necessary to search in different places than was the case thirty years ago. Private homes, attics, basements, and barns are no longer the primary sources for American country antiques. People in the remotest of hamlets are aware of general values and usually do not encourage strangers knocking on their doors. Many collections or accumulations that would have been offered at a backyard sale twenty-five years ago now make their way to highly visible auction houses.

The number of antiques shops has diminished due to increasing overhead and the evolution of "antiques" malls in every other abandoned grocery store or gas station in North America.

There is also an abundance of antiques and collectibles shows every weekend in most urban areas. A growing number of shows tend to specialize in a specific type of antique, ranging from glass and jewelry to Americana and advertising. "Tailgate" shows, set up in as close as proximity as available to a major show, bring a crowd from diverse geographical areas. The dealers who set up at the "tailgate" shows often have comparable merchandise to the dealers at the more prestigious event, but do not have to fight the heavy booth rent and related costs. A generation ago collections were often put together from shops, but the declining number of antiques emporiums has turned much more attention to shows as a primary source for major purchases.

Collections of painted furniture three decades ago were relatively few and even farther between. Often a collector had to convince a shopkeeper not to strip the original finish on a cupboard or bucket

Arched trellis covered with trumpet vine serves as an entry way to a stone house in Amana, Iowa.

bench before he could race across town or the state to take it off the dealer's hands. Refinished pine covered with a dressing of shellac was much more coveted at that point.

Age and condition were the commonly used adjectives to describe the object of most affections. Surface was a term that seldom was discussed because it wasn't an issue. If an item was painted, it was typically stripped, sanded, steel wooled, and then "finished" In most cases removing an original painted surface tended to hurt the piece because significant time and effort had to be expended to separate the aged surface from the wood hiding under it.

In our books we have always attempted to include country antiques that a semi-serious collector could uncover with some perspiration and time. Thirty years ago "primitive" collectors from California to western Ohio had to embark on sometimes lengthy field trips to find much of consequence. Today there are probably as many collectors and dealers traveling east to west on buying trips. All sections of the nation have selected shops, shows, and malls that feature American country antiques.

Some of the items that decorate the pages that follow possibly would not have been considered worthy of adding to a collection a generation ago, but as you surely know by now, things change.

An oversized grinding stone used to sharpen farm tools and implements in Amana, c. early 1900s.

Lilies, holly hocks, and a potpourri of herbs surround another Amana, Iowa home.

Painted wheelbarrow filled with geraniums.

6

Stone that has been hollowed out to serve as a water or food container for chickens, c. early 1900s, found in Kentucky

Miniature windmill, c. 1940, found in southern California.

Wire plant stand, painted green, c. 1920 with geraniums.

Early twentieth century farm wagon from central Illinois.

Child's wagon from c. 1940 loaded with a garden box filled with geraniums.

Red poppies from a garden in eastern Iowa.

Bittersweet wreath and Christmas garlands of selected herbs.

White graniteware pitcher, c. 1920, filled with larkspur.

Contemporary log cabin birdhouse, found in central Illinois.

Sometimes the sign leads to a rare bargain and other times it brings about anxiety and despair.

Detailed birdhouse on an overcast December morning in rural Illinois.

Pumpkins and gourds can be found in quantity and variety at every outdoor market in middle America in August, September, and October.

Pine and maple wheelbarrow with remnants of its original paint.

Chapter 1
Kitchen Antiques

Among Americana collectors, one of the most significant changes that has come about over the past twenty-five years is the intense interest in maintaining the original finish or surface on any item that is under consideration for adding to the permanent collection. It doesn't make any difference if it is a pie safe or a wooden chopping bowl, the original worn or painted surface is a critical factor in the evaluation and acquisition process. Price, size, condition, and provenance are essential ingredients in the mix, but if the surface has been repainted, refinished, or rearranged the check usually will not be written.

As the interest in original painted surface has grown and prices have soared, a number of semi-skilled "artists" have picked up brushes to add a new finish to old pieces with the intent of deceiving collectors. This problem has been compounded by the influx of kitchen and hearth "antiques" from Europe, Mexico, and South America that are legitimately old, but not nearly as "American" in origin as described on the price tag.

Factory-made butter mold of maple, c. late nineteenth century.

The design on this butter mold was mechanically impressed into the steamed maple surface of the print.

Uncommon cow design on c. 1880-1910 butter mold, factory-made.

Collection of butter molds and prints and other examples of nineteenth century woodenware. Maple was commonly used for nineteenth century kitchen implements because it was a hard wood, easily cleaned and didn't flake or splinter after prolonged contact with liquids.

Collection of butter molds and prints in a painted bowl from Pennsylvania.

Sugar buckets with "fingers" and copper nails, c. late nineteenth century. It is a fairly common practice to call anything with "fingers" and copper nails "Shaker," but there are numerous factories that used this particular style in their manufacturing of wooden buckets.

Staved wooden sugar bucket with wooden bands and handle, painted a mustard color, c. late nineteenth-early twentieth century.

Red factory-made bucket with wooden "drop" handle that carries the hand lettered "Ginger" to denote its contents.

Rare blue painted miniature bucket with wire "drop" handle, 5" diameter of lid.

Green sugar bucket with "fingers" and iron nails. Like most utilitarian pieces that have survived, sugar buckets and any other kitchen related antique should show signs of wear. The paint on this bucket could not possibly be pristine unless it had been recently repainted.

Stack of four late nineteenth-early twentieth century sugar buckets.

"Lipstick" red bucket with "fingers" and copper nails.

Three painted buckets and small chest with its original painted surface.

Miniature sugar bucket with "fingers," staved construction, wooden bands, and wire "drop" handle with a maple grip.

Early twentieth century bucket with paper "P.J. Ritter's Apricot" label.

"Preserved Golden Drop Plums" bucket in gray paint, c. early 1900s.

Early twentieth century painted sugar bucket with wire "drop" handle and original painted finish.

Four painted sugar buckets showing the type of consistent wear that a collector would expect to find.

Stack of buckets on "lipstick" red bench.

Shaker oval box in blue paint. The distinguishing characteristics of a Shaker box are an oval shape, "finger" construction, copper nails, maple sides, and a pine top and bottom.

Shaker 6" oval box, New England, c. 1880.

Shaker box in dark blue paint. The purpose of the fingers was to control the expansion and contraction of the wood over time and prevent cracks, The copper nails didn't rust and discolor the wood.

Shaker box with "Harvard" fingers.

Shaker 10" box with a stained rather than painted surface.

Shaker cheese box with "button hole" hoops and mustard paint.

Shaker storage tub with iron bands, staved construction, blue exterior paint and white interior paint.

Shaker box in green paint. The boxes were sold individually or in nests of 6-9 over a long period of time with little change in design or construction.

Berry pails sold in the New England Shaker community gift shops to visitors during the late nineteenth-early twentieth century.

Shaker berry pail with "diamond" shaped braces supporting the "drop" handle.

Shaker berry pail with blue exterior and white interior paint.

Close-up of Shaker berry buckets.

Collection of berry pails ranging from 3" to 6" in diameter.

Shaker berry pails with original painted surface. The pail at the
right has a 9" diameter.

Shaker covered pantry box with diamond braces and "drop" handle with blue painted surface.

Another staved blue bucket with wooden bands. Note the difference in the way the bands are used to keep the staves tightly bound together. This bucket is still water tight after more than a century.

Staved bucket with wooden bands and blue paint.

Blue staved butter churn with metal bands and original lid and dasher.

Dasher butter churn with strong blue paint that dates late nineteenth century and was found in central Illinois.

Nineteenth century butter churn with "piggin" handle and wooden bands.

Factory-made Blanchard butter churn #5 in mustard paint, c. 1915.

Staved sap bucket with metal bands, paint of indeterminate age. When sap buckets make their way to market, they are typically found in large quantities because of a warehouse or factory find when a 100 or more are discovered.

Painted pantry boxes and pantry boxes with "drop" handles, factory-made.

Large measure in bittersweet paint, c. early twentieth century.

Collection of buckets in "as found" condition.

Bittersweet staved bucket with metal bands and "drop" handle.

Factory-made measure in original stained finish, early 1900s.

Two lathe-turned maple "work" bowls in original painted finish. In recent years the interest in painted bowls has increased significantly. The price structure for bowls has followed the growing demand and enhanced the potential for profit by adding what appears to be century old paint to unpainted bowls.

Collection of painted bowls, sugar buckets, and pantry boxes.

Collection of painted bowls ranging from 5" to 35" in diameter

Cherry knife and fork box with dovetailed sides and original blue painted surface, c. mid-nineteenth century.

Painted spools from New England textile mills, maple, c. 1880-early 1900s.

Stack of painted factory-made pantry boxes from the early 1900s.

26

Collection of nineteenth century spinning wheels and yarn winders.

Painted wooden wheelbarrow with cast iron wheel, c. 1920s.

Tiger maple butter worker, New England, nineteenth century.

Factory-made spice box with original lettering and porcelain drawer pulls, c. 1915.

Handmade four drawer spice chest of pine with original painted finish, c. 1870.

Painted wall box, pine, square nail construction, leather hinged storage area, c. mid nineteenth century.

Factory-made barrel churn with original base, staved construction with metal bands, c. 1900.

New England scrubbing stick for cleaning clothes, c. mid-nineteenth century.

Yellow staved barrel with metal bands, c. 1930.

Green oak barrel, staved construction with metal bands, c. 1930.

Brass kettle with 22" diameter and "drop" handle, American, c. 1870s.

Green painted shutters taken from central Illinois home built in the 1850s.

Cast iron kettle with "drop" handle, c. late nineteenth century.

New Hampshire churn and butter worker, original blue paint, c. 1860s.

Leather fire bucket, original paint, gold lettering and numbers, c. 1850, New England.

Painted tin candlebox, c. mid-nineteenth century.

Shaker-made oval keeler, staved construction, 36" diameter, New England, nineteenth century.

Painted and decorated pine shoeshine box, c. early 1900s, found in North Carolina.

Collection of copper, brass, and tin ladles and skimmers, nineteenth and early twentieth century.

Sliding lid pine box with lollipop handle, original finish and carved finger pull, signed "Elias Sloat, Born Dec. 4th 1726".

New England pine hanging candle box in original red canted front Fire bucket from Nantucket, Mass. Hour glass with blue/green glass sections joined with cloth and wax at waist, 18th century oak frame.

Chapter 2
Stoneware

Stoneware is primarily a product of the nineteenth century. Its demise was brought about by the growing influence of home refrigeration and the inexpensive production of glass containers. The stoneware potteries that survived into the twentieth century molded their wares rather than throwing each piece individually on a potter's wheel. Collectors today are chiefly concerned about the cobalt decoration on a piece, the maker's mark, the form of the piece, and its condition.

Stoneware was a utilitarian product that was used extensively throughout the United States in rural and urban areas. Collectors today can find surviving pieces almost anywhere but seriously decorated examples are rare. It has been our experience that the single best source for purchasing stoneware is from dealers who specialize in it. They are the most familiar with current market trends and usually price their wares accordingly.

The more elaborately decorated pieces were seldom made in large quantities and are especially difficult to locate today.

Decorated stoneware falls into a category of collecting that produces competition between folk art enthusiasts and stoneware collectors. The result is inflated prices for exceptional examples.

Ovoid or pear shaped jug with brushed floral decoration, c. early 1840s.

Late nineteenth century vendor's jug with slip-trailed address.

Ovoid two gallon jug with brushed decoration, c. early 1840s.

Late nineteenth century midwestern cooler with slip trailed decoration.

Ovoid jugs from New York State, c. 1830s-1840s.

New York state vendors's jug with stenciled decoration, c. 1880s.

Cylindrical sided jug with deep cobalt decoration, c. 1870s-1880s.

Ovoid two gallon jug, c. 1830s.

Greensboro, Pennsylvania, stoneware jug with stenciled decoration, c. 1870s.

Contemporary double handled jug, made by Crocker and Springer of Elsah, Illinois, 1994.

Late nineteenth century six gallon crock with stenciled capacity mark and decoration, midwestern in origin.

New York state two gallon crock with slip-trailed and brushed cobalt flower, c. 1870s.

Midwestern five gallon crock with slip trailed decoration, c. 1880s.

Heavily decorated New York state crock, c. 1870s.

Three gallon crock, midwestern, slip-trailed decoration, c. 1880s.

Two gallon crock, New Hampshire, c. 1870s-1880s.

Five gallon midwestern crock, slip-trailed insect and capacity mark, c. 1880s.

Unmarked crock with simple brushed cobalt flower.

Utica, New York elaborately decorated cobalt bird on a branch, c. 1870s.

New York state, vendor's crock, cobalt stenciled information, c. 1880s.

New York state vendor's crock with intense cobalt inverted "Christmas tree" or "tornado" decoration, c. 1870s-1880s.

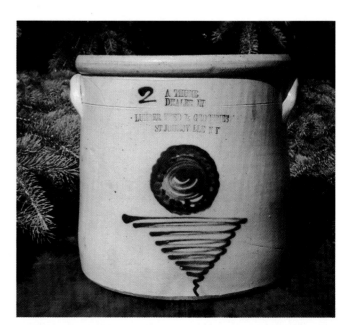

New York state two gallon crock with floral decoration, c. 1870s.

Greensboro, Pa. stoneware jar with stenciled decoration, c. 1880s.

Macomb, Illinois four gallon churn made for Louesia Avery, c. 1880s, slip-trailed decoration.

Greensboro, Pa. two gallon jar with brushed and stenciled decoration, c. 1880s.

Unmarked western Pennsylvania canning jar with stenciled decoration, c. 1880s.

Unmarked Pennsylvania canning jar with brushed decoration, c. 1870s-1880s.

Contemporary stoneware jar from Crocker and Springer, Elsah, Illinois 1994.

Two gallon jar, dated "1870", slip-trailed.

Unmarked two gallon jar, midwestern, c. 1880s-1890s, slip-trailed.

Greensboro, Pennsylvania, three gallon jar, slip-trailed and brushed decoration, c. 1870-1880s.

Two gallon stoneware jar with brushed flower, c. 1870s.

Brush decorated cake or butter crock, Pennsylvania, c. 1860s-1870s.

Brush decorated stoneware pitcher from Pennsylvania, c. 1860s-1870s.

Undecorated stoneware pitcher from New York state, c. 1870s.

Elaborately decorated Pennsylvania pitcher, c. 1860s-1870s.

Midwestern stoneware crocks, stenciled decoration, c. 1920-1930.

Eight gallon stoneware crock with stenciled decoration, maker's mark, and capacity mark, c. 1920s-1930s.

Six gallon crock, midwestern in origin, c. 1920s-1930s.

Molded stoneware dog from Ripley, Illinois, c. late nineteenth century.

In the late nineteenth century there was a revival of interest in completing art or craft projects at home. This child's "memory" jar involved covering a stoneware jar with soft clay and impressing into the surface small toys, teeth, keys, and marbles.

Collection of molded "blue and white" stoneware pitchers and salt crocks, c. early 1900s.

48

Collection of molded early twentieth century mixing bowls.

Molded stoneware mixing bowls, c. 1880-1920.

Sponge decorated molded stoneware pitcher, midwestern in origin, c. 1880s.

Molded stoneware jug from Peoria, Illinois Pottery, c. 1905.

Molded stoneware chimney from Cincinnati, Ohio, c. late nineteenth century.

White Hall, Illinois Pottery "Beater Jar", molded with Bristol glaze, c. 1915.

Molded stoneware White Hall, Illinois jar with sponge decoration, c. early 1900s.

Blue Band two gallon butter churn, c. early 1900s.

Two gallon Red Wing, Minnesota butter churn, c. 1900.

Molded mugs, midwestern, c. early 1900s.

Three gallon Smithville, Mississippi butter churn, c. 1900.

Molded pitcher, midwestern, c. early 1900s.

Pig with a map of the Illinois Central Railroad incised into it,
Anna, Illinois, c. late nineteenth century.

Molded "Sleepy Eye" pitcher, Monmouth, Illinois Pottery, c. 1930.

Peoria Pottery molded canning jar, c. 1905.

Slip-trailed duck and slip-trailed bird on a branch from New York state, nineteenth century.

Opposite Page: Row of molded early twentieth century stoneware offered at a midwestern antiques market.

Heavily decorated nineteenth century stoneware crock, jug, and jar from New York state, and Bennington, Vermont.

Chapter 3
Country Furniture

The next time you attend a heavily promoted antiques show that features dealers who specialize in Americana, make it your mission to pay special attention to the furniture offered for sale. American country furniture that still carries its original surface is a tough ticket to find in today's market.

Thirty years ago dealers, collectors, or pickers who knocked on doors or attended rural auctions could occasionally buy furniture that was still part of the family for whom it was originally constructed. These houses have since been torn down to make way for another video store or tanning salon.

Most handcrafted pieces of country furniture were made before 1880. After that date furniture factories were mass producing oak parlor and bedroom suites for a growing population with an unquenchable appetite for goods that weren't "homemade."

The pine cupboard or poplar pie safe ended up on the back porch or in the basement to hold several

Pine pie safe with turned legs, replaced screen wire, and painted surface, c. late nineteenth century.

generations of canned garden vegetables or motor oil. Inevitably the painted surface was worn away, the tins on the pie safe rusted out, and the furniture was turned into kindling.

Stoneware was impervious to moisture and could emerge from a half century's sleep in the basement unscathed. Baskets and butter molds easily fit into boxes in the attic and could also be stored with little difficulty. But furniture was subject to wear and loss.

The aforementioned trip to the antiques show should result in a surprising amount of quality "smalls" and a consistently dwindling supply of country furniture.

A search for a legitimately blue pie safe with pierced eagle tins in the doors could turn into a lifelong quest. If you are in need of a poplar pie safe with traces of faded red paint, rusted tins, and a replaced drawer, don't forget to bring along the station wagon and $600.

Pine, poplar, and walnut jelly cupboard, midwestern, c. 1880.

Child's step-back cupboard in original salmon paint, missing center drawer, 38" x 24" wide, c. 1900.

Factory-made kitchen cabinet, maple and poplar, probably never painted, refinished, c. 1915.

Factory-made poplar and pine kitchen cupboard, c. early twentieth century, worn white overpainted surface.

Grained jelly cupboard, pine, c. 1870s, original hardware and finish.

Midwestern pine pie safe, worn red paint and original pierced tins, c. late nineteenth century.

Factory-made kitchen storage cupboard, pine and poplar, c. early 1900s.

Blue jelly cupboard, pine, c. mid-1800s, painted basket and boxes, early 1900's hooked rug.

Painted storage cupboard with cut-out legs, unusual cast iron hardware, probably New York state or Pennsylvania in origin, c. mid-1800's.

"Fire house" Windsor or lodge hall chair, factory-made, c. early 1900s, remnants or original finish and stenciling, maple, pine, and hickory.

Collection of spindle-back chairs with pine plank seats, c. 1915, factory-made.

Adirondack chair with original splint seat and back, c. 1900.

Adirondack rocking chair, original splint seat and back, c. early 1900's.

Painted ladder back side chairs with finials and replaced splint seats, c. mid-nineteenth century.

Wicker arm chair, repainted surface, c. 1920s.

Boston rocking chair with original paint and grained finish.

Collection of wicker furniture with new paint, c. 1920s-1930s.

Child's high chair, spindle-back, splayed legs, replaced foot rest, c. 1860, original paint, found in Ohio.

Nineteenth century side chair with ladder-back, turned finials, original splint seat and blue paint.

Factory-made kitchen chairs with early painted surfaces, c. late nineteenth century.

Refinished ladder-back side chairs with replaced rush seats, and turned finials, nineteenth century.

Early nineteenth century child's rocking chair, ladder-back, replaced fabric seat, worn painted finish.

Lyre-back kitchen chair with original painted decoration and stenciling, c. 1880s.

Set of four late nineteenth century painted kitchen chairs, replaced rush seats, ladder-backs.

Mt. Lebanon, New York Shaker rocking chair, ebony finish #7 in size, replaced rush seat, c. 1900.

Early twentieth century kitchen chairs, pine plank seats, overpainted, spindle backs.

Shaker ladder-back chair used for sorting apples, original finish, replaced seat, two Shaker footstools with replaced tapes, c. 1900.

Half-spindle backed side chairs in worn original painted finish and stenciling, factory-made, c. 1870s.

Oak grained pine lift top desk, used on a counter, c. late nineteenth century.

Set of four kitchen chairs with rush seats and original stenciled decoration, factory-made, c. 1880s.

Painted blanket or six board chest with turned feet, c. 1840s, pine, New England.

Dome top trunk, grained surface, original hardware, c. 1840s, Rare six board chest with splayed sides, dry red paint, pine, New England in origin, c. 1830.

Maple factory-made stool in "lipstick" red paint, c. early twentieth century.

64

Maple bed side table with turned legs, c. 1850.

Four drawer pine chest with turned maple pulls, c. mid-nineteenth century.

Dome top storage trunk, painted decoration, iron lock, c. 1840-1860.

Painted lift top blanket chest, single drawer, turned legs, c. 1860.

Painted storage box, 16" x 8" x 10", found in New York state, c. mid-nineteenth century, pine.

Pine hanging shelf with two dovetailed drawers, original painted surface, c. 1860's.

Pine chest. painted green with nailed sides, original condition, c. mid-nineteenth century, 14" x 7" x 6".

Pine drop leaf table, painted blue, c. mid-nineteenth century.

Pine and ash wood box, worn original surface, c. early 1900s.

Pine bucket bench, original painted surface, top dovetailed to the sides, found in Indiana, c. mid-nineteenth century.

Refinished pine and maple table, turned legs. c. late nineteenth century.

Pine and maple rope bed, painted with turned "urn" posts, c. 1850.

Pine wash bench, painted finish with a scrubbed top, "boot jack" legs, c. late nineteenth century.

Refinished pine jelly cupboard, c. late nineteenth century.

Pie safe, painted green with original screen wire, late nineteenth century, found in Indiana.

New England sack-back Windsor arm chair, c. 1775, original Windsor green paint, bulbous turned legs and arm supports, found in New York City.

Slat-back arm chair, c. 1780, scrolled arms, acorn finals, crusty black paint over orange, Bergen County, New Jersey.

Wear on stretchers and leg bottoms of the Windsor chair. It is highly unusual for a Windsor chair to survive with its original painted surface intact.

Close up of slat-back arm chair's acorn finial.

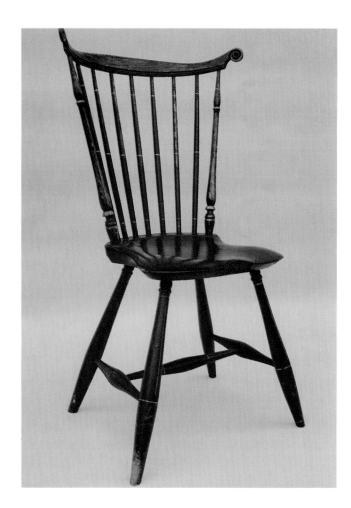

Late 18th century fan-back Windsor side chair from Rhode Island, original black paint over grey wash, bulbous turned stiles and partially turned legs with an exaggerated saddle seat.

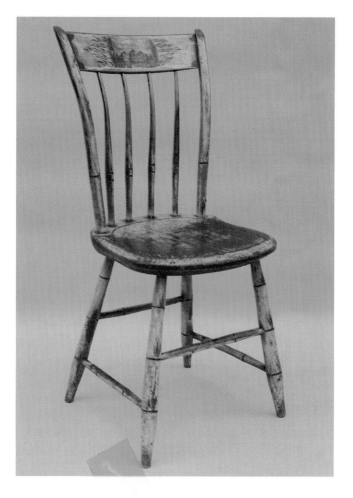

Sheraton Windsor side chair in original yellow paint and decoration, c. 1820-1830.

Arrow-back Windsor rocker, c. 1820-40, with grain painted finish that was added in the late nineteenth century, found at an estate auction in Illinois.

Child's settle bench with storage below seat, pine with old patina, traces of black paint, rose head nail construction, c. 18th century, found in western Massachusetts.

Crest rail of yellow Sheraton Windsor reported to be showing Boston buildings destroyed by the British.

Queen Anne side chair, Eastern Shore, early 18th century, old dark finish over traces of red, original seat with bold ring and ball front stretcher turnings, from Old Deerfield Academy, Old Deerfield, Massachusetts.

Hudson River Valley Queen Anne side chair with pad (duck) feet, old refinishing with early replaced rush seat, c. 1740-1760.

Trumpet foot of early 18th century Queen Anne chair.

New England late 18th century sack-back Windsor armchair, old black paint, found in eastern Connecticut.

Connecticut seven spindle fan-back Windsor side chair, branded "JDN", 18th century original dark surface, purchased in Vermont.

Close up of Connecticut sack-back Windsor showing simple turned leg, "alligatored" black crusty surface over red.

Shield shaped seat of Connecticut fan-back showing exceptional wear. Generally Windsor legs are wedged on the top section (inside) of the leg but this chair also employed rose head nails from the top section of the seat.

Bannister-back arm chair, c. 1750-60, tombstone crest and "elephant" arms, original ball feet, early 19th century grain paint, found in New Hampshire.

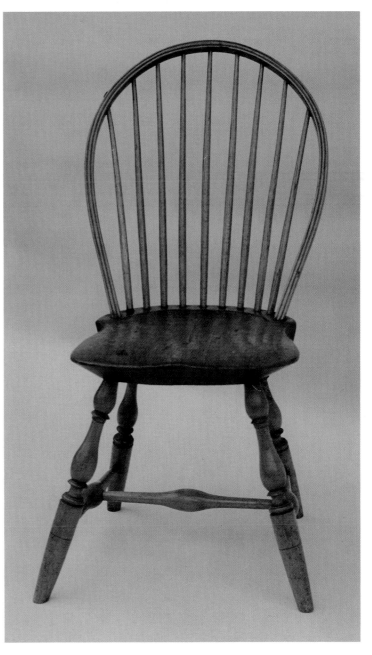

New England, 9-spindle Windsor bow-back side chair.

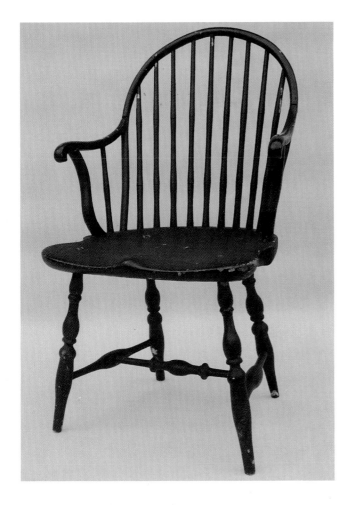

Rhode Island bow-backed Windsor arm chair, late 18th century, serpentine arms and supports, old black over red.

73

Well developed and strong turnings on legs of the bow-back which support a thick, deeply chamfered seat, old refinishing has developed a soft mellow color.

Pine server with shaped gallery above two framed doors over a simple bracket-footed base, original grey blue surface, probably New England in origin, found in Illinois.

Queen Anne child's blanket box with early 18th century construction, original painted salmon surface, snipe hinges, applied molding on the base.

New England tap table with single drawer, one board top with bread board ends on all four sides, original apple green surface, c. 1800, found in Maine.

Rare Windsor stool, late 18th century with pine top and hickory turned legs, old finish with no signs of ever been painted, found in Connecticut.

Lancaster County, Pennsylvania dough box on splayed turned legs with half ball feet, single drawer with added Bennington pull, dovetailed case, poplar with original brown over red wash, c. 1760-1780.

Pine black and red grained painted one drawer stand with tapered legs, early 19th century, probably New Hampshire in origin.

Old grunge finish on the one drawer stand showing wear on table top edges.

Queen Anne child's blanket box on well scrolled base, original brown surface covers dovetailed construction, original snipe hinges, found in Quechee, Vermont.

Ohio or Kentucky three shelf bucket bench with half circle cut out sides, original red surface with top shelf plate groove.

New England, paint decorated 18th century candlestand, red top and turned shaft painted red and green, three legged base is painted red.

Virginia Eastern Shore one door cupboard with interior shelves, replaced H-hinges, old red surface with grey paneled door, yellow pine construction.

Portrait of a boy in a blue dress holding a book in original gilt frame, c. 1820-1840. Two drawer blanket chest, c. 1680-1700, New England.

Refinished ladder back chair with original splint seat, c. late nineteenth century.

Child's fireside settle bench, pine, c. nineteenth century.

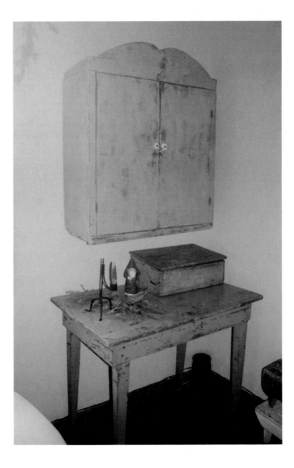

Pine hanging cupboard and simple pine table with two board top, c. nineteenth century.

Pine and maple step-back cupboard with glazed front, refinished, c. 1880, midwestern in origin.

Pennsylvania low-post bed, pine and maple, original painted surface, nineteenth century.

Chapter 4
Country Store Antiques

Unlike most categories of Americana, examples of country store and advertising antiques can be found almost anywhere. During the summer of 1994 we had the opportunity to purchase the contents of a rural grocery store that had been closed in the 1940s when the elderly owner died with no apparent heirs. The store generated little interest for almost fifty years until the area around it began to be surrounded by an upscale housing development at which point it was rediscovered and offered for sale. Unfortunately, most of the contents had been semi-devoured by mice or rust and emerged into the sunlight with limited value.

Ornate display cabinet decorated with a collection of women's hats, c. 1920.

Oak display cabinet filled with an assortment of early twentieth century products.

A cupboard or dry sink can have a damaged leg or door and with expert repairs still maintain much of its value. Advertising that has been repaired, repainted, or refinished loses almost all of its interest to serious collectors. Condition is absolutely critical in establishing the worth or marketability of a particular piece. This problem is compounded because most of the pieces of advertising initially were thought to have minimal value and have survived, not out of love, but through luck or being stored away and simply forgotten.

Collection of signs and six pristine coal shovels.

Collection of tobacco products and counter.

Cans and boxes of early twentieth century food related items.

Late nineteenth century cast iron store scale in original painted and stenciled surface.

Seed salesman's sample case, c. 1900.

Collection of early twentieth century seed boxes.

Sioux City, Iowa seed box, early 1900s.

Page's Seeds counter display with metal exterior logo, c. early 1900s.

Ezra Williams, Rochester, New York seed box with paper labels, c. 1880s-1890s.

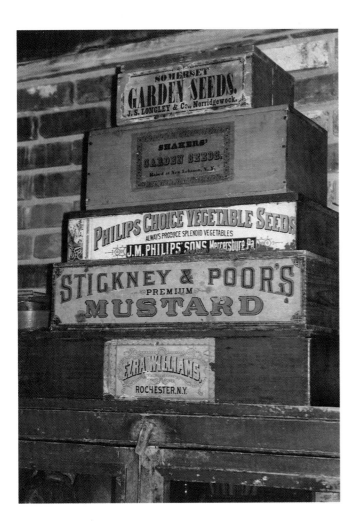

Collection of seed boxes and a Stickney and Poor's mustard box.

Oversized W.B. Burt seed packets, c. 1915.

Unopened seed packets from Hiram Sibley & Company, c. early 1900s.

Seed jar from a midwestern hardware store with a pouring spout in the lid, c. 1930s.

Cast iron coffee mill #3 from the Enterprise Company.

Cast iron coffee mill #2 from the Enterprise Company of Philadelphia, Pennsylvania, c. 1890 with original painted and decal decoration.

Cast iron Grand Union Tea Company "home" coffee mill, c. early 1900s, original painted surface.

Cast iron counter coffee mill with original paint and hopper, c. 1880s.

Elgin National Coffee Mill #42, c. early 1900s.

LaFendrich Cigar advertising thermometer, c. 1920s.

Coffee mill, machine dovetailed box with cast iron top, c. 1920s.

"Cafe" sign, 42" x 36" wide, found in western New York, c. 1930s, original painted surface.

Tin on pine frame, "Apartment for Rent" sign from New York City, c. 1920s.

Cast iron American eagle from entryway to 1930s Oklahoma gas station, 37" tall, original worn painted surface.

Case Eagle, 9' tall, made from fiber glass and originally attached to the front of a tractor dealership in central Illinois, c. early 1950s.

Detail of cast iron American eagle (top left)

Oasis Cigarettes almost life size advertising camel from the 1930s, found in northwestern Ohio.

Snow Drift Flour barrel lid from Grand Rapids, Michigan, c. 1910 with paper advertising.

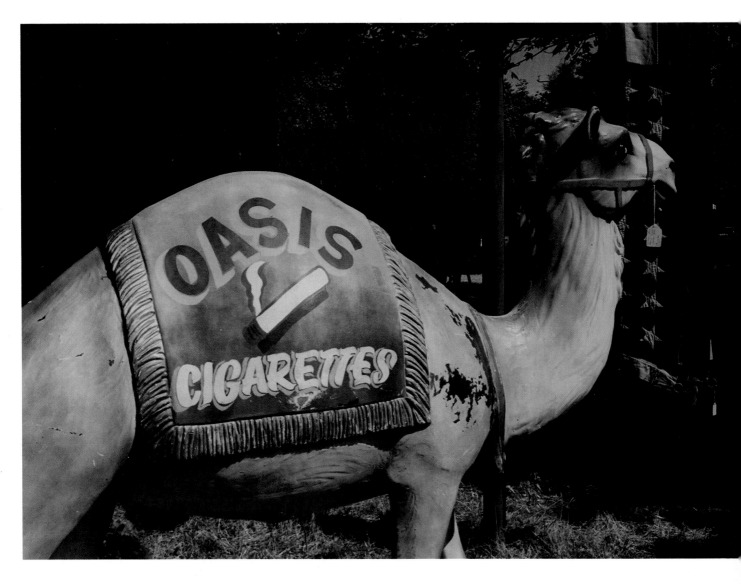

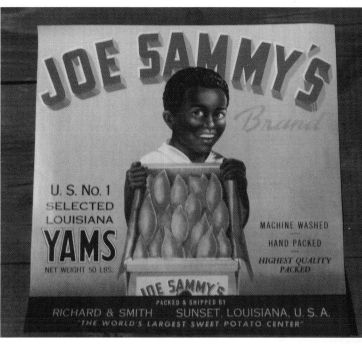

"Joe Sammy's" label from 1940s yams box.

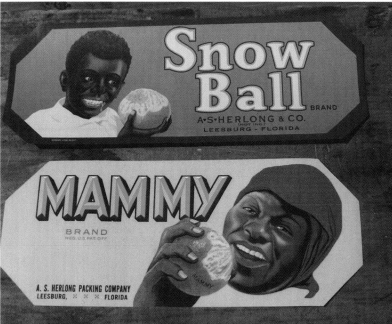

Carnival sideshow sign, probably 1930s, found in Ohio, 48"
tall.

Unused orange crate labels, c. 1930s-1940s.

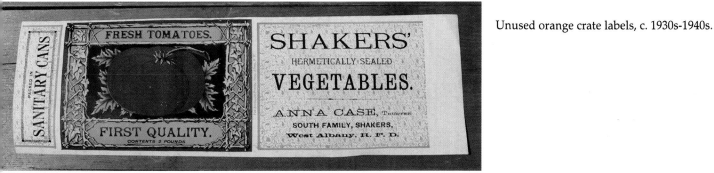

Unused can label from "Shaker's Vegetables" c. early 1900s.

Sweet Cuba Tobacco counter container, c. early 1900s.

Grocery store roasted coffee bin, c. 1880-1900 found in Lancaster County, Pennsylvania.

Cross Cut Cigarettes advertising chair with scenes of an African-American couple courting and their marriage in original condition, c. 1890.

Blue Tip match 1¢ dispenser, c. 1940.

Union leader tobacco paper "stand up" for use on a counter or shelf.

Bull Dog Cut Plug tobacco tin, early 1900s.

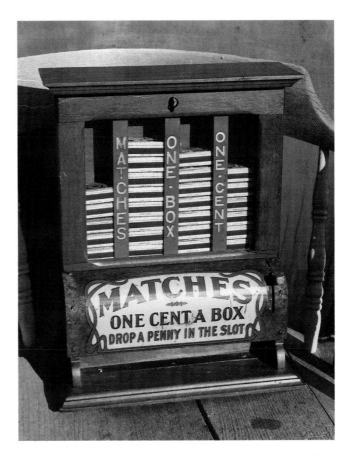

1¢ match dispenser in original condition, c. 1910.

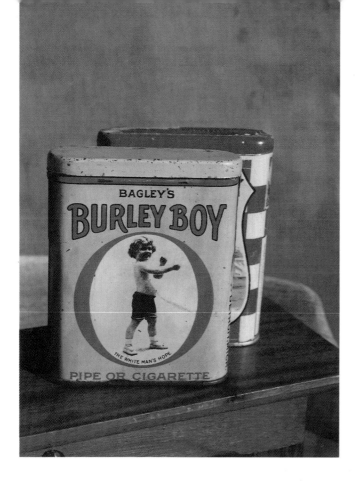

Bagley's Burley Boy tobacco tin, c. 1920.

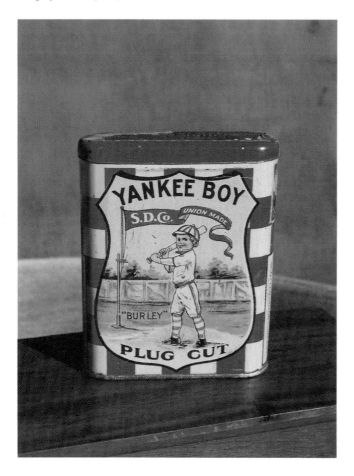

Rare Yankee Boy Plug Cut tobacco tin, c. 1920s.

Underwood Talmage candy bucket with paper label, c. early 1900s.

Old Dutch Cleanser store display, c. 1930s.

Blue Diamond "stand up" advertisement, c. 1920s-1930s.

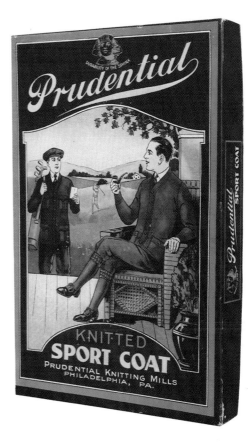

Prudential Sport Coat box, c. 1920s.

Ramsfleece Underwear box, c. 1940.

Cloverbloom Butter boxes, c. 1930s.

Shaker Salt packing box, c. early twentieth century, machine dovetailed.

Prima Donna Soap counter display box, c. 1900.

Keen's Mustard box with paper interior and exterior labels, c. 1920.

Potato chip case, found in western Ohio, c. 1920s.

Six drawer spice chest with original paint and lettered drawers, early 1900s.

Rare five drawer spice chest with original paint and lettered drawers, early 1900s.

Parts storage case for DeLaval Cream Separators with metal exterior label and oak case, c. 1915.

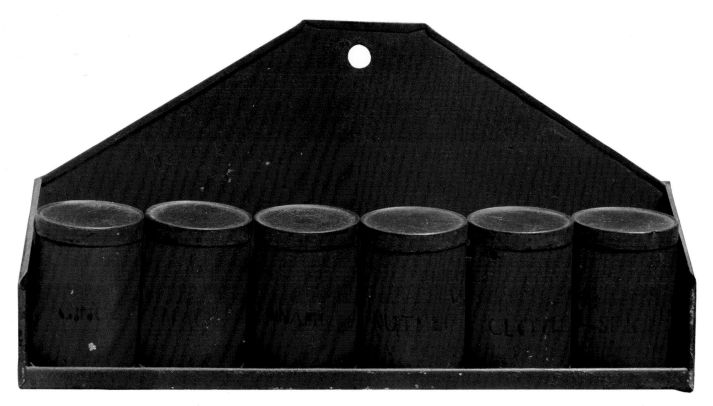

Set of spice boxes and holder, original brilliant red paint, c. 1920s.

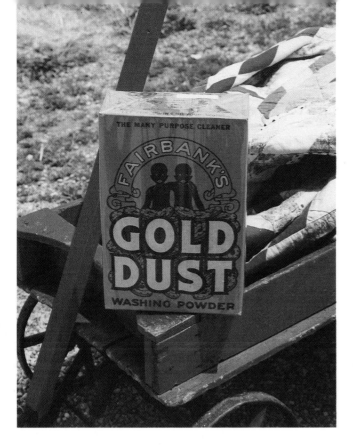

Gold Dust Washing Powder box, c. 1930s.

Collection of meat cleavers from a 1920s grocery or butcher's shop.

St. Regis shaving brushes in original display case, c. 1910.

U.S. Mail Soap box and painted pine Brach's Candies display table, c. 1930s.

Preserves bucket with "drop" handle, brilliant blue paint and remnants of a paper label, c. early 1900s.

George Washington chain pump in original stenciled case, c. 1910.

Six milk crates in original condition, c. 1950s. These are still available in almost limitless quantities today but eventually they will disappear and be desirable.

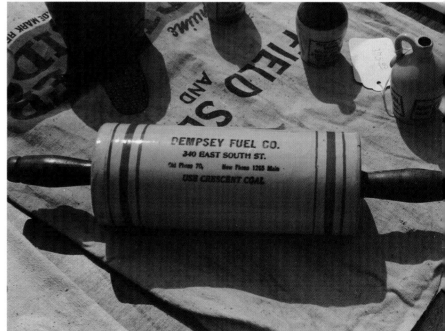

Stoneware rolling pin with maple handles with advertising for the Dempsey Fuel Company, probably given away as a Christmas premium to customers, c. 1900-1910.

Six boxes of Fountain Youth mineral water crystals, c. 1930s.

Buck Beverage Company case with strong blue paint and
stenciled lettering, c. 1920s.

Shaker pickles bottle with original paper labels and stopper, c. 1900.

Shaker horse radish bottle with original paper label, late nineteenth century.

The condition of the paper labels is exceptional.

Blown nineteenth century jar filled with Noils Mohair, found in Pennsylvania.

Pennsylvania rye straw basket used to allow dough to rise.

Splint utility basket with carved handle.

Splint flower gathering basket, found in Illinois.

Early twentieth century splint flower or garden basket.

Collection of splint baskets, first half of twentieth century.

Willow fishing creel with leather binding and hinged lid for storing the catch of the day, twentieth century.

Willow fishing creel, c. 1880s.

Fishing creels, wicker with leather trim, twentieth century. Nineteenth century creels tend to be flatter in form and made of woven splint with a wooden hinged lid.

Late nineteenth century Shaker sewing basket, New England, form sold in the visitors' shops, 13" diameter.

Nineteenth century miniature splint basket with a bitter-sweet paint and black brushed decoration, 4.5" diameter.

Backside of Shaker sewing basket.

Miniature buttocks basket with twisted oak handle, rib construction.

Fruit or utility basket, splint 14" diameter.

Splint egg or utility basket with a "kick up" bottom to distribute the weight of the contents.

Melon basket, rib construction, splint.

Native American utility basket, splint, 5" x 8".

Painted utility basket, splint.

Painted bushel basket with "kicked in" bottom to distribute weight of fruits or vegetables, found in New England.

Splint utility basket with carved oak handle.

Tightly secured handle and wrapped rim of the painted bushel basket.

Extremely well-made wash or clothes basket, found in Illinois, c. early twentieth century, 40" handle to handle.

Painted New England egg basket with "drop" handle, found in New Hampshire.

Interior view of the wash basket.

Nantucket "lightship" basket, c. early 1900s, rattan with turned wooden bottom. Crew members from the "lightships" anchored off Nantucket Island made baskets with rattan imported from southeast Asia and sold their work to tourists. Most of the baskets date from about 1850 to 1920. They were often made and sold in sets of up to eight baskets of graduated size.

Turned wooden bottom of the Nantucket basket.

Woven willow field or gathering basket, nineteenth century, found in southern Alabama.

Wall or half basket, rib construction, splint, c. early 1900s.

Apple picker's basket with oak grip and splint loops to secure a belt, found in New York state.

Miniature melon basket, rib construction, splint, found in Pennsylvania, nineteenth century.

Willow magazine stand, c. 1930, factory-made, found in New York state.

Painted utility basket with carved oak handle, tightly woven, c. 1900.

Group of Nantucket baskets (left to right): late nineteenth century 6" round with wooden ears; light ship basket 7.5" diameter, signed "William P. Sandsbury", c. 1890-1900; basket signed "Mitchell Ray", 20th century, 11.5" wide; small oval 6.75" signed "Mitchell Ray, Nantucket, Mass", early 20th century; medium sized oval 9.5" basket attributed to Appleton, c. 1900.

Buttucks basket, rib construction, made from willow, c. early 1900s.

Collection of three early 20th century baskets, found at rural home near Watseka, Illinois.

Chapter 6
Toys

Over the years we have occasionally collected toys without a significant amount of attention paid to their condition. If the toy had the "look" that we liked, we usually bought it. Once or twice, out of ignorance, we actually found something that was rare and offered to us at a reasonable price by a seller who was equally uninformed.

Several years ago, in Seattle, we purchased a Schoenhut Humpty Dumpty Circus tent, and a representative sampling of the animals, equipment, and personnel that originally accompanied it. Instantly our toy buying perspective changed and we began to view toy collecting much more seriously.

Unlike the blue step back cupboard of our dreams, toys can turn up almost anywhere. They can be uncovered in a long forgotten attic in Utah or at a Wednesday flea market on Route 1 in southern Maine.

The rules that apply to the serious evaluation of any other classification of country antiques should apply equally to toys. These would include:
1. Original condition
2. Age
3. Quality of the painted surface
4. Degree of rarity
5. Price

Painted pine game board, c. nineteenth century, found in New England, 16" x 24".

Early twentieth century game board, painted pine, found in Indiana, 10" x 10".

Unusually decorated game board, painted, c. 1920s, 36" x 36".

Steiff dog pull-toy.

German feather tree, cobalt blue dyed feathers, turned pine base, 18" tall, c. 1920s.

Horse pull toy, pine platform, iron wheels, c. early 1900s, probably German in origin.

Circus clown/acrobat, carved pine, nineteenth century.

Pull toy on painted platform, metal wheels, c. 1920s.

Folk art Uncle Sam doll, c. 1930s.

Horse pull toys on painted bases, probably German, c. early 1900s.

1940s factory-made horse, found in Danville, Illinois, original painted finish and detail.

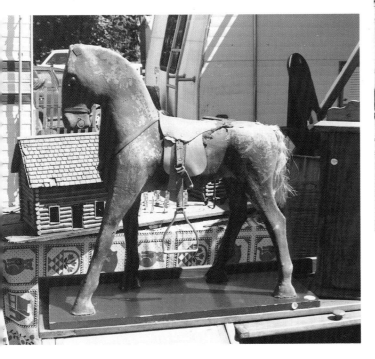

Rocking horse on replaced base, hide over pine, c. early 1900s.

Infant's rocking bird toy, pine, original painted finish, c. 1920s.

Late nineteenth century framed valentine with paper message. found in Pennsylvania, 3.5" x 4".

Noah's ark, probably German in origin, original painted finish, 18" x 8", complete with 37 animals and two human figures, c. late nineteenth century. Arks were especially popular in late nineteenth century homes that prohibited children from playing with toys on the Sabbath. The biblical connection with Noah and the ark opened the door for parents to allow their children time with animals, people, and the boat on Sundays when the other toys were off limits.

Pennsylvania doll cradle with heart cut out, nailed corners, original paint, pine and walnut, c. mid-nineteenth century.

1920s watermelon serving dish.

Contemporary folk art watermelon.

Roulette wheel game of chance with race horses and jockeys, c. 1940.

Child's delivery wagon, wooden wheels with iron rims, c. early 1900s.

Freehand lettering indicating that the wagon belongs to "Joe".

Painted wagon, original condition, c. 1925.

Unusual smiling Jack-O'-Lantern with original paper lining, c. 1940s, and carbon residue left from burning candle.

Child's Jack-O'-Lantern, metal with hand-painted decoration, interior candleholder, and stick, c. 1920s. This Jack-O'-Lantern was used much like a parade torch with a carrying stick. It was factory-made and sold during the first quarter of the twentieth century.

Rare skeleton lantern from the 1940s with wire handle.

The Jack-O'-Lanterns were made of molded and compressed cardboard and were placed with a candle inside on a window sill or carried by candy gatherers on Halloween night.

Collection of three Jack-O'-Lanterns and a cat lantern from the 1940s-1950s.

Another Jack-'O-Lantern made of molded and compressed cardboard. This one used by candy gatherers on Halloween Night.

The lanterns were sold in dime stores for .15-.40 cents during the 1940s and 1950s. It is difficult to find the lanterns in perfect condition because they were in heavy use each year on October 31.

Miniature Jack-O'-Lantern, 4" diameter, stem, c. 1950s.

Gourd grown in Illinois with 35" diameter carved into a Jack-O'-Lantern.

Cardboard rabbit candy container, c. 1930.

Unusual devil Jack-O'-Lantern with original paper liner, c. 1950.

Paper candy box with Santa Claus, 9" diameter, c. 1915.

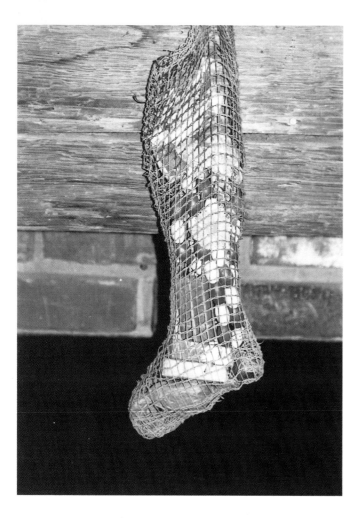

Christmas sock filled with inexpensive children's toys from the 1920s and never opened.

Child's hooked mitten, found in Maine, c. early 1900s.

Collection of worn and well loved Teddy bears, c. 1930s-1940s.

Dolls from the 1920s.

The A. Schoenhut Company of Philadelphia began making the Humpty Dumpty Circus in 1903 and continued until the factory closed in 1935. Schoenhut created animals, circus personnel, tents, and equipment.

Clown with original Schoenhut Humpty Dumpty Circus box.

Clown from the late 1920s.

Clown wearing costume decorated with multicolored card suits.

The Schoenhut Ring Master.

Clown with costume decorated with red stripes and dots on a white field.

The Hobo.

Painted eye two-humped or Bactrian camel.

Lady Circus Rider with bisque head.

Giraffe with wooden dowel horns, leather ears, and a woven cord tail.

The "extra-fine" elephant with a howdah blanket and triangular headdress with gold ric-rac or fringe.

Painted eye tiger.

The olive brown painted surface was applied to the donkey through a dipping process. There was an "extra fine" donkey that came with a felt saddle edged with gold ric-rac or trim.

Leopard with woven cord tail and yellow body with brown stenciled spots.

Glass-eyed white horse with oval saddle.

The lion.

Monkey with red felt costume, wire tail covered with woven cloth, and a felt hat.

Goat with leather tail, whiskers, horns, and ears.

Painted-eye poodle.

Humpty Dumpty Circus personnel, equipment, and animals.

Clown with multicolored plaid costume and painted eyes.

Doll purchased for Edna Goley Faulkner on her first birthday in Dupo, Illinois in 1912.

Pair of late nineteenth century dolls.

Collection of late nineteenth century-early twentieth century marbles.

Child's farm wagon in original painted condition, Harvard, Illinois, c. early twentieth century.

Chalk cat and chicken and horse pull toy on wheeled pine platform.

The three bears, c. 1920s.

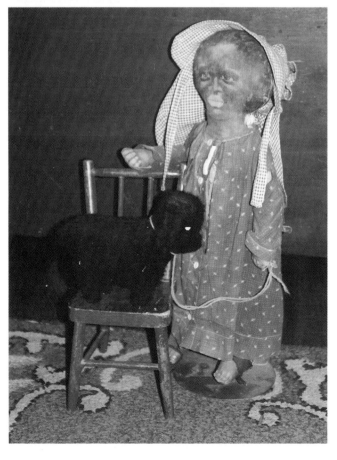

Early twentieth century cloth doll made from a pattern.

Twentieth century folk art doll.

Chapter 7
"A Little Bit About a Lot of Things"

When we began to collect American country antiques thirty years ago, we were fortunate to gain some direction from several couples who had been down many of the roads we were beginning to travel. They independently suggested to us that we should not limit our interests to candlemolds or pine furniture, but we should seek anything that caught our collective eye and fit our relatively thin checkbook. They all agreed that if you see something great, have the means to buy it, and a way to get it home, you will eventually find somewhere to put it.

In the mid-1960s most people were not paying a significant amount of attention to painted furniture, decorated stoneware, advertising and other examples of Americana. There were not an abundance of antiques shows, markets, and malls to attend. We traveled from shop to shop around the middle of America and periodically had some success in uncovering something we could not live without.

About an hour from our home was the small central Illinois village of Melvin that contained a restaurant which offered a Friday night buffet in Tupperware for a dollar and an antiques shop located in the former office of the local doctor. The doctor's widow went to farm auctions and house sales to occupy her time and offered her purchases for a few dollars more than she had paid for them.

Brass and iron skimmer, Pennsylvania, c. 1860s.

Cast iron kettle, c. mid-nineteenth century.

The Friday night procedure was always the same. After we had the $1 buffet we would go down the block to the shop and she would show us the week's acquisitions. Invariably she would say "This time I have got a little bit of a lot of things. Right now you don't understand what this is, but fifteen years down the road you'll love it." She would then show us a chrome yellow blanket chest with a grained finish that most dealers would have already stripped.

"Now I paid a lot of money for this and it took $2 worth of gas to drive out there, but I knew the family and its been in that house for a 100 years. If you want it, you can have it for $48. If it's good, it's always going to be worth the money so you better buy it." We always did.

This chapter is a little different than the rest of the book because it is not as focused as the previous sections on specific categories of country antiques.

Compare it to the antiques shop in Melvin. It's got "a little bit of a lot of things."

Collection of tin food molds and kitchen utensils, late nineteenth century.

Cast iron door stop, c. 1940.

Cast iron farm implement seat, painted surface, c. 1930s.

Painted calf and cow bells found in Texas, c. early 1900s.

Cast iron cat door stop, original painted surface, c. first half of the twentieth century.

Cast iron rabbit door stop, original painted surface, found in eastern Iowa, c. 1930s.

Collection of early twentieth century graniteware.

Rare cobalt graniteware coffee pot, c. 1900.

Collection of grey graniteware, c. 1930.

Blue graniteware coffee pot, c. 1930.

Garden watering can and child's graniteware milk jug for school lunches, c. 1930.

Watering can from a 1930s gas station with painted bittersweet surface. This watering can is an example of a $15 piece with a $60 paint job.

Unusual sprinkling can with the notation "A Present For William", found in New York state, c. early 1900s.

Nineteenth century tin coffee pot in original condition.

Nineteenth century blown glass storage jars with tin lids.

Blue painted New England metal sap bucket, early 1900s.

Copper apple butter kettle, 44" diameter, iron "drop" handle, found in southern Illinois, c. 1900, dovetailed bottom and sides.

Copper apple butter kettle with 26" diameter.

Rooster windmill weight, "Woodmanse", Elgin, Illinois.

Rooster windmill weight, "rainbow tail", made by the Elgin (Illinois) Wind Power and Pump Company, c. early 1900s.

Bull windmill weight, Fairbury Windmill Company, Fairbury, Nebraska, made between 1910 and 1920.

The Fairbury bulls were originally painted a bright red. This example has been repainted at some point and the farmer's initial "R." has been added. This weight was found at a farm sale in western Iowa.

This Eclipse is called a "wet" moon because the points go toward the heavens. The much less commonly found "dry" Eclipse has the points hanging down.

Eclipse crescent moon governor weight, made by Fairbanks, Morse and Company, Chicago, IL.

Ellipsoid or "football" shaped counter-balance weight, made in Evansville, Wisconsin between 1915-1920.

Althouse-Wheeler Company counter-balance windmill weight from Waupun, Wisconsin. The "W" was painted black at the factory but, as is the case with most weights, the lengthy contact with the weather has taken the paint away.

Cast iron hitching post, numerous repaints, c. early twentieth century.

French nineteenth century clock weight.

Cast iron horse's head hitching post, c. early twentieth century.

Painted pine bird house, c. 1940.

Pine 1940s bird house.

Unusual painted bird house from the early 1900s, found in Vermont.

Buggy wheel, c. 1915.

Wheel from c. 1915 farm wagon with original hub and weathered surface.

Felt pennant with sewn on letters, c. 1930s.

Felt pennant with sewn on letters from the 1930s.

Storage house for garden implements, 40" x 36" x 44", c. 1920. This house was used to store lawn and garden tools on a suburban Chicago estate. The roof lifts off.

Midwestern quilt, c. 1920.

Dated "1924" hooked rug with animals, 42" x 32".

1930s comforter from northern Indiana.

Collection of hooked rugs offered for sale at midwestern antiques market.

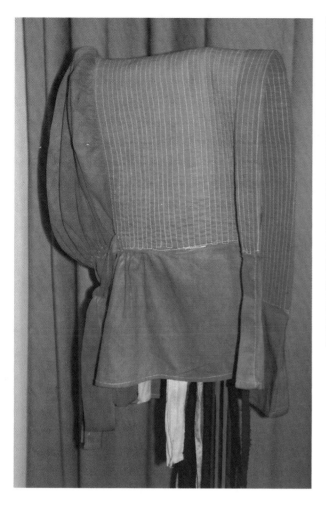

Cardboard box filled with contemporary duck decoys.

Late nineteenth century midwestern bonnet.

Collection of 1920s-1950s hats.

Chapter 8
Country Christmas

Americans have a natural and national tendency to keep Christmas decorations and ornaments long after they have outlived their usefulness. They are stored carefully away until a "next year" that may not come until the estate sale when they are rediscovered in a festive box under a worn quilt in the attic. This gives Christmas antiques and collectibles collectors a unique advantage because some very good things turn up in unlikely places.

In June 1988 we attended the sale of the home and contents of baseball Hall of Fame member Ed Roush in Oakland City, Indiana. Among the chairs, tables, brooms, garden hose, and farm wagons loaded with a lifetime of accumulation was a 40" German feather tree in pristine condition with its original stenciled base. The people at the sale expressed little interest in the feather tree when its turn to be auctioned arrived so we were pleased to buy it for $35.

In mid-December, 1994, we went to St. Charles, Illinois to wind our way through the antiques shops and malls. One especially dreary mall was located on a busy street surrounded by discount stores. The business was packed with jelly glasses, 1940s furniture, *Life* magazines from the 1960s, oil paintings from an abandoned Holiday Inn and a 35" Santa Claus doll stuffed with straw and still in full Christmas Eve dress uniform. The doll dated from about 1910 and was hidden behind a velvet and plastic depiction of Elvis in Las Vegas during his robust period.

The discovery of Santa Claus made the excursion a meaningful Christmas experience for both of us.

Contemporary folk art angel, c. 1994.

Section of a 4' x 4' oilcloth with holiday scenes used to surround the base of the Christmas tree each year, c. 1900.

Decorated German-made feather Christmas tree with original stenciled pine base, 40" tall, c. 1915.

5' Santa Claus doll from the 1940s with rare cobalt feather tree and painted and turned base, imported from Germany for the American market, c. early 1900s.

Collection of decorated "bottle brush" Christmas trees, c. 1940s-1950s.

Window sill filled with variety of "bottle brush" Christmas trees.

35" tall Santa Claus doll filled with straw, c. 1910, original condition.

Santa Claus with candle light, found in Waynesville, Ohio, c. 1940s.

Feather Christmas tree, 48" tall, c. early 1900s, German in origin.

Santa Claus candy container filled with c. 1940s Woolworth's artificial Christmas tree.

"A Merry Christmas" postcard sent to "Dad" from "Chester" in Merna, Illinois, December 22, 1903.

Turned wooden bowl filled with dried fruit and evergreens.

Crab apples in a covered pantry box with a "drop" handle.

Birdhouse with a shingled roof, pine scrubbed top table, Christmas greens.

Grape vine Christmas wreath carved bird and greens.

Painted maple bowl, fruits, and greenery.

Contemporary Windsor chairs, nineteenth century step-back cupboard, and Christmas decorations.

Twenty gallon stoneware crock filled with holly and pine branches.

Hanging glazed front cupboard with red paint, found in Vermont, c. mid nineteenth century.

Scrubbed top table with storage shelf, hanging spice box, and greenery.

European goat cart decorated with Christmas greenery.

Turned wooden bowl filled with apples, nuts, potpourri, and candles.

Birdhouse constructed to resemble an ark, found in Illinois, c. 1930.

Collection of Santa Claus figures and candy containers,
twentieth century.

Child's blocks, c. early 1900s and pewter.

100 TL	100-150	BL	50-75	TR	800-1000	BL	650-875	ML	75-100	B	25-50 ea.
TR	225-275	TR	75—100	BL	425-500	BR	300-350	MR	75-100	153 TL	375-500
BL	100—200	BR	40-75	122 TL	175-200	132 TL	150-175	BR	100-150	TR	250-300
BR	200-300	112 BL	125-175	TR	300-350	TR	400-500	144 TL	250-300	BL	25-50 ea.
101	350-425	BR	150-200	BL	100-150	BL	150-175	TR	200-250 ea.	154 TL	350-450
102 TL	450-600	113 TL	125-200	BR	300-350	BR	400-500	BL	20-40	TR	200-300
TR	600-800	TR	600-800	123 T	250-350 ea.	133 TL	400-450	BR	300-500	BL	500-700
B	150-200	B	350-450	BL	300-450	TR	375-450	145 TL	200-300	BR	200-225
103 TL	55-75	114 MR	225-250	BR	100-125	ML	325-400	TR	800-1000	155 TL	10-12
TR	15-20 ea.	BL	200-250	124 TL	225-225	MR	400-475	BL	1200-1500	BR	75-150
BL	325-475	BR	150-200	TR	100-150	BR	350-375	BR	400-600	156 TL	1500-2000
BR	50-75,	115 T	150-200	B	900-1500	134 TL	125-175	146 TL	400-600	BR	350-450
	200-225	BL	100-150	125 TL	200-275	MR	450-525	TR	150-175	157 TL	400-500,
104 TL	350-400	BR	300-375	TR	25-50	BL	400-475	BL	150-175		300-475
TR	350-450	116 TL	300-400	B	225-275	135 TL	350-425	BR	200-400	TR	250-350
BL	10-15 ea.	TR	75-100	126 T	500-600	TR	500-575	147 TL	500-800	BL	300-400
BR	200-250	MR	275-350	M	175-300	BL	350-400	TR	500-800	158 T	50-150 ea.
105 T	4-6 ea.	BL	500-600	127 TL	450-600	BR	250-325	BL	300-400		
B	100-150	117 TL	850-1100	BL	250-350	136 TL	150-200	BR	200-250		
106 TL	400-500	M	250-350	TR	300-500	137 TL	400-500	148 TL	95-135		
TR	300-400	BL	100-125	BR	100-125	BL	1200-1600	TR	50-75		
BR	200-300	118 TL	350-500	128 TR	200-250	138 TL	300-600	BL	125-200		
107 TL	600-750	M	250-300	BL	200-250	139 TR	150-225	BR	75-100		
R	300-450	BL	75-125	BR	50-75	BL	150-200	149 TL	75-100		
BL	300-350	BR	300-400	129 TR	75-100	141 TL	100-125	TR	60-75		
108	400-500	119 T	850-1750 ea.	BL	200-250	TR	50-60	BL	600-900		
109 BL	150-200	BL	100-150	BR	75-100	BL	50-100 ea.	150 TL	300-375		
110 BL	400-600	BR	75-150 ea.	130 TL	125-150	BR	150-250	TR	300-400		
TR	125-150	120 TR	300-350	TR	125-175	142 TL	250-350	BL	100-150		
TL	400-475	BL	250-300	B	200-300 ea.	BR	350-400	151 TL	100-150		
111 TL	85-100	121 TL	500-600	131 T	85-150 ea.	143 TL	250-350	TR	25-50 ea.		

Holly leaf Christmas wreath.

Scrubbed-top pine harvest table with drop leaf, painted base, found in Ohio, c. 1870.

Price Guide

The prices stated below reflect items in at least "excellent" condition with no major structural flaws. The prices reflect what one could realistically expect to pay at retail or auction. The lefthand number is the page number. The letters following indicate the position of the photograph on the page:

T = top
B = bottom
BL = bottom left
BR = bottom right
TL = top left
TR = top right

L = left
R = right
M = middle

The right hand numbers are the estimated price ranges.

Page	Pos	Price	Page	Pos	Price	Page	Pos	Price	Page	Pos	Price	Page	Pos	Price	Page	Pos	Price
7	BL	200-275		B	350-450 ea.		BR	200-300	56	TB	500-600	68	T	250-400	85	T	4000-6000
	BR	700-900	25	B	300-400 ea.	39	TL	250-300		BL	400-500		BL	400-500	86	MR	300-400
11	BL	100-125	26	M	300-375		BL	400-600	57	TL	350-450		BR	600-800		BL	300-400
	BR	250-300		BR	2800-3200		TR	225-300		TR	500-700	69	TL	2800-3500	87	TR	250-275
13	TL	300-500	28	TL	250-300		BR	300-375		BL	300-350		TR	2000-2500		BR	325-375
	TR	275-350		BL	200-250	40	T	225-300		BR	650-850	70	TL	2600-3000	88	T	250-300
	BL	275-350		TR	150-200		M	250-300	58	TL	400-600		TR	650-850		B	350-450
	BR	350-400		BR	250-300		BL	350-400		TR	300-400		BL	800-1100	89	TR	12-15 ea.
14	TL	300-350	29	TL	150-250	41	TL	150-175		BL	800-1100		BR	2200-2600		B	15-20 ea.
	TR	275-325		BL	200-250		TR	300-500	59	TL	75-100	71	TR	3800-4500		MR	25-35
	BL	300-375		TR	150-200		B	300-350		TR	50-75		BL	1200-1500		BR	25-35
	BR	1400-1700		BR	150-200	42	TL	500-600		BL	150-200	72	TL	2000-2600	90	TL	500-700
15	T	300-350	30	TL	50-100		BL	150-200		BR	150-200		TR	1500-2000		TR	500-700
	BL	250-300		BL	75 ea.		TR	375-450	60	TL	125-150 ea.	73	T	3500-4500		BR	400-500
	BR	300-350		TR	100-150		BR	400-600		TR	150-250		M	1000-1200	91	TL	500-675
16	TL	300-350		BR	75-100	43	BR	200-250		BL	350-400		BL	3000-4000		BL	650-800
	TR	200-250	31	TL	300-400	44	TL	200-250	61	TL	200-250	74	TR	1500-2000	92	TL	100-125
	BL	1400-1700		TR	400-500		TR	50-75		TR	250-275		BL	1500-2000		TR	200-300
	BR	1600-2000		BL	300-350		BL	200-250		BL	125-150 ea.		BR	2200-2600		BL	300-450
17	T	800-950		BR	500-700		BR	200-250		BR	125-150 ea.	75	T	2500-3000		BR	200-250
	M	650-850	32	TL	100-150	45	B	300-350	62	TL	150-250		MR	2700-3200	93	TL	2500-3000
	B	650-850		BL	800-1200	46	TL	300-400		TR	100—150		ML	1200-1600		TR	600-1000
18	T	400-475		BR	800-1200,		TR	75-100		B	800-1000 set	76	TL	1200-1600	94	TL	1000-1200
	M	600-700			1200-1500,		BL	50-75	63	TL	1600-1800		TR	2500-3000		TR	200-300
	BL	400-500			800-1100		BR	200-250		TR	35-50 ea.		BL	1750-2200	95	TL	600-800
	BR	350-400	33	L	300-350	47	T	50-150 ea.		BL	800-1000		BR	1200-1700		TR	12-15
19	TL	400-450		R	125-150		BL	40-50		BR	100-175 ea.	77	T	6000-8000,		M	12-15
	ML	400-500	34	TR	300-400		BR	50-100 ea.	64	TL	800-1000 set			13000-15000		BL	150-225
	BL	300-400		B	300-400 ea.	48	TL	125-175		TR	350-400		B	75-125	96	TL	225-350
	TR	1200-1500	35	TL	125-175		TR	2000-2400		MR	400-600	78	TL	400-600		TR	400-500
20	T	1500-2000		TR	200-250	50	BL	225-275		BR	350-450		TR	400-500		BL	1000-1500
	B	350-400 ea.		BL	250-300		BR	50-75		BL	75-100		BL	1200-1600	97	TL	250-350
21	TL	350-400		BR	200-300	51	TL	125-150	65	TL	250-350		BR	800-1000		TR	150-200
	TR	200-250	36	TR	150-175		TR	200-250		TR	300-400	82	B	500-650		BL	250-300
	BL	150-200		B	300-375		BL	125-175		B	275-350	83	TR	400-475		BR	350-500
	BR	400-500	37	TL	150-175		BR	100-150	66	TL	600-800		MR	300-400	98	TL	400-550
22	TL	400-500		TR	300-400	52	TL	300-350		TR	250-300		BR	1200-2000		TR	400-600
	TR	400-450		BL	125-150		TR	40-50 ea.		ML	400-500			ea.		BL	500-700
	BL	250-300		BR	200-275	53	T	4000-6000		MR	250-300	84	TL	1500-2000		BR	300-475
	BR	50-75	38	TL	125-150		B	350-400 ea.		B	600-700		TR	1200-1500	99	TL	100-125
23	BR	300-350		BL	200-300	54	TL	25-50	67	TL	300-375		ML	1600-1800		TR	65-75
24	TL	100-125		TR	125-150		TR	500-700,		TR	700-800		MR	400-500		BL	75-95
	TR	50-75		MR	350-475			600-800		BR	500-600		B	500-600		BR	50-60